BRITAIN IN OLD PHOTOGRAPHS

OXFORD

YESTERDAY & TODAY

MALCOLM GRAHAM &

LAURENCE WATERS

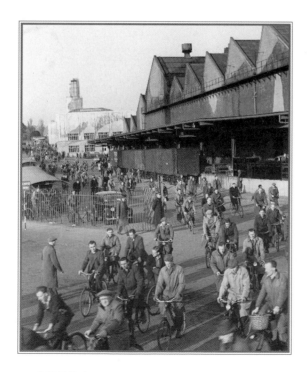

SUTTON PUBLISHING LIMITED

Sutton Publishing Limited
Phoenix Mill · Thrupp · Stroud
Gloucestershire · GL5 2BU

XFORDSHIRE BOOKS

First published 1997

Reprinted in 2002

Copyright © Malcolm Graham & Laurence
Waters, 1997

British Library Cataloguing in Publication Data
A catalogue record for this book is available from the
British Library.

ISBN 0-7509-1303-7

Typeset in 10/12 Perpetua.
Typesetting and origination by
Sutton Publishing Limited.
Printed in Great Britain by
J.H. Haynes & Co. Ltd, Sparkford.

CONTENTS

Introduction & Acknowledgements		4
1.	Principal Streets	7
2.	North-West of Carfax	21
3.	North-East of Carfax	41
4.	South-East of Carfax	59
5.	South-West of Carfax	69
6.	Jericho & North Oxford	81
7.	St Clement's & East Oxford	93
8.	South & West Oxford	103
9.	The Oxford Villages	113

INTRODUCTION

Matthew Arnold's Scholar Gipsy looked down on Oxford as 'That sweet city with her dreaming spires' and visitors from all over the world come to see a place which promises to whisper from its towers 'the last enchantments of the Middle Age . . .'. Against all the odds that image still has some substance but, if Oxford has not been broken by the forces of change, it has certainly had to bend before them.

At the beginning of the nineteenth century Oxford had a population of about twelve thousand living within the bounds of the medieval town; a hundred years later, in 1901, the city housed nearly fifty thousand people, many of them in what Gerard Manley Hopkins described as a 'base and brickish skirt' of Victorian suburbs. Now, Oxford has a population of over 136,000 and, having incorporated ancient villages and former countryside within its boundaries, the city covers more than 11,000 acres (4,500 hectares).

The scale of this growth, fuelled by industrialization in the twentieth century, has inevitably brought change to the city and its setting. Fields have been transformed into suburbs, meadows have become industrial estates, small shops have given way to larger units and under-used land has been subject to more intensive development; moreover the continuing growth of the university and colleges has had an obvious impact on the city and its suburbs. It may now be harder to detect the Christminster of Thomas Hardy's *Jude the Obscure* in the hectic modern city, but we should perhaps be surprised and not a little grateful that so much of old Oxford has survived. The fact that colleges are major landowners has certainly helped to preserve crucial areas and the Thames and Cherwell flood plains have deterred some developments. At the same time, the planning process, encouraged or cajoled by local groups and individuals, has been generally successful in resisting the most harmful schemes and channelling development into more appropriate areas. Visitors to Oxford may no longer be able to see the city's towers and spires from Iffley Road or Banbury Road, but the strategic purchases of the Oxford Preservation Trust since 1926 have helped to save many views that might otherwise have been lost. The Trust has also been influential in the struggle to preserve the individual character of Oxford's villages.

The motor industry brought a new prosperity to twentieth-century Oxford but the city, like everywhere else, has had to adapt to the age of personal mobility. Quiet streets where grass proverbially grew during the Long Vacation were soon filled with local and long-distance traffic, creating a need for the Ring Road and other relief roads, road widening schemes and the provision of parking spaces. Road improvements tried to keep pace with increasing demand until the 1960s, but two controversial schemes, the Christ Church Meadow relief road and the Eastwyke Farm road, were defeated and the City introduced a Balanced Transport Policy in 1973. Park and Ride buses and bus lanes have encouraged the use of public transport and limited the growth of traffic in the city, but factors such as rising car ownership, bus deregulation, changing patterns of shopping and long-distance commuting are beyond local control. The Oxford Transport Strategy currently envisages a greater degree of pedestrianization in the city centre.

Until the 1960s much of central Oxford had an air of picturesque decay because the Headington stone used on many of its historic buildings had weathered so badly. This undoubtedly gave the place an antique charm and Nikolaus Pevsner, for example, wanted to retain the old Emperors' Heads in front of the Sheldonian Theatre because 'This "ragged regiment" is by now in such a wonderful state of decomposition and ought to remain so.' They were replaced in 1972, however, and extensive restoration work by the university and colleges, helped by the Oxford Historic Buildings Fund between 1957 and 1974, has transformed the appearance of the city centre.

Older town houses in Oxford were traditionally seen as expendable in the face of college or commercial development and, ironically, it needed the outbreak of the Second World War to save the Broad Street/Ship Street block from imminent demolition. Thomas Sharp recognized the townscape value of vernacular houses as a foil for grander buildings in 1948 and the Pembroke College North Quad in 1966–7 was an early instance of practical conservation, restoring and incorporating fine old properties in Pembroke Street.

Slum clearance has been one of the most controversial policies in twentieth-century Oxford. Arising out of the urgent and understandable wish to do something about appalling housing conditions in areas like St Ebbe's, St Thomas's and the surrounding villages, wholesale clearances decanted communities to distant housing estates and destroyed historic as well as substandard houses. Local pressure and the City's eventual change of heart helped to preserve much of Jericho from a similar fate and, since the 1970s, new housing has been bringing people back to some of the cleared areas.

No age was ever truly golden and comparison between the old and new photographs in this book reveals plenty of gains as well as losses. Oxford is still a city to be savoured and enjoyed, a place which was described by Henry James as 'The finest thing in England'.

THE PHOTOGRAPHS

The oldest photographs in this collection date from about 1860 but the pace of change has become so fast that some of the 'old' photographs were only taken twenty or thirty years ago. As a photographer it is always interesting when looking at old photographs to speculate about the type of camera and negative material that was used in capturing the images. Many of the early shots in this book were taken using large plate cameras supported by heavy wooden tripods, the glass negatives requiring long exposures. These cameras were not very manoeuvrable and took some setting up, attracting crowds of onlookers in areas where a photographer was quite an novelty. To replicate some of these shots by setting up similar equipment in the middle of today's busy streets would mean risking serious injury and, for ease of use, the new photographs were taken using modern 35mm equipment.

In order to minimize obscuring effects of leaf cover and to make the book as up to date as possible the new photographs were taken between November 1996 and January 1997. During the winter the sun is low in the sky and, on clear sunny days, it throws heavy shadows. In order to show as much detail as possible many of the pictures were taken on bright overcast days; in these conditions, soft lighting gives good detail and allows the camera to be pointed in any direction without the problems of shooting directly into the sun. All of the images were shot on Ilford HP5 film and were processed with the development time slightly extended to increase the negative contrast.

The book is arranged so that the reader begins in the city centre and fans out through the surrounding suburbs to the villages that have become part of Oxford since 1929. The first section covers the heart of the city, the four main streets centred on Carfax; the next four sections take the form of strolls around the north-west, north-east, south-east and south-west quadrants of the city centre. Sections six to eight extend into the city's nineteenth-century suburbs, looking at Jericho and North Oxford, St Clement's and East Oxford and, finally, South and West Oxford. The last section covers Oxford's villages, following a clockwise arrangement from Old Marston round to Wolvercote.

ACKNOWLEDGEMENTS

Most of the old photographs in this book are from Oxfordshire County Council's Photographic Archive but we are indebted to the following for permission to reproduce their photographs:

Jeremy Daniel: top photographs on pp. 86, 89
Oxford & County Newspapers: top photographs on pp. 26, 32, 26, 70, 71, 79, 82, 92, 98, 99, 137; & p. 42

PRINCIPAL STREETS

The High, 1920s

Customers gather round a coffee stall at Carfax early one morning, *c.* 1900. Slatter and Rose's shutters were still up but Gill's the ironmongers encouraged window shoppers with eye-catching displays and two suspended baths. On the left, a Walton Manor Dairy milk cart has been parked beneath the projecting lamps.

The exuberant Lloyd's Bank building (1900–1) rounded off the north-east corner of Carfax and the bank now occupies Gill's old shop which was part of Sainsbury's Oxford store until 1973. The quarterboys on Carfax Tower, modern replicas of seventeenth-century originals, look down on a busy junction.

Advanced jaywalking in a High Street filled with vehicles during the Silver Jubilee, 1935. On the left, Hall's the tailor's was flourishing and rival music businesses, Russell's and Acott's, occupied premises on either side of the Westminster Bank. On the right, three taxis occupied a rank inherited from the days of horse-drawn cabs.

Traffic still dominates High Street and taxis still wait outside the former All Saints' Church, now a library for Lincoln College. The buildings are virtually identical but Russell's merged with Acott's beyond Alfred Street and the National Westminster Bank expanded into its old shop.

Six women cyclists and their dog enjoy the freedom The High Street, early 1920s. This view, looking past The Queen's College towards All Souls' College and St Mary the Virgin Church, demonstrates the gradual curve which Wordsworth described as 'the stream-like windings of that glorious street'.

The view remains the same in almost every detail but there is usually less opportunity to enjoy it. Pedestrian refuges were introduced in the centre of the High Street in the 1930s and there are now two crossings controlled by traffic lights. A car free, carefree High Street is promised by the Oxford Transport Strategy.

The Angel Inn, High Street, mid-1860s. First recorded as the Tabard in 1391, the inn was enlarged in 1510 and was renamed the Angel. It became Oxford's most important inn during the coaching era and, in about 1830, nine coaches left there every morning at 8 a.m. Queen Adelaide, consort of William IV, stayed at the Angel in 1835.

The Angel lost its coaching trade with the coming of the railways and the inn closed in 1866. The University's Examination Schools (1876–82) occupied much of the site but, owing to divided property ownership, two bays of the Angel survive as 83–4 High Street. Frank Cooper's famous Oxford Marmalade was first sold at no. 84 in about 1874.

Silver Jubilee decorations outside Grimbly Hughes' grocery store in Cornmarket Street, 1935. The view includes the long frontage of the Clarendon Hotel and, on the right, part of the roof of Buol's, a popular Swiss restaurant. Traffic here, including a lorry bound for Osberton Radiators, was coming to dominate the shopping street.

The face of Cornmarket Street was radically changed in the 1950s and 1960s by the building of large new stores for Woolworth's, Marks & Spencer and, nearestto the camera, Littlewoods. Cornmarket Street was closed to most traffic in 1971 but the halfway house to pedestrianization is visibly imperfect.

The northern end of Cornmarket Street and Magdalen Street from the corner of Ship Street, August 1907. A sandwich-man outside Charles Underhill's wine shop advertises a sale and a London & North Western Railway parcels van approaches George Street. In Magdalen Street, Elliston and Cavell's store was enjoying years of expansion.

Continuity is much more evident at the top end of Cornmarket. Two former pubs, the Plough and the Northgate Tavern, survive as shops and the same lamp bracket still lights the St Michael's Street corner. The most striking change is perhaps St George's Mansions next to George Street, which was described as Oxford's first skyscraper in 1910.

Queen Street, 1907, looking towards Carfax and the distant spire of All Saints' Church. A lively scene with shoppers on the pavement and a woman cyclist outside Frederic Sellers' grocer's shop; by the Oxford Dairy Co. a man is sluicing down the pavement with the help or hindrance of two lads.

The half-timbered former Morris Garages showroom on the extreme left (1910) has looked down on a partially pedestrianized Queen Street since 1970. Large-scale developments have included the Marks & Spencer store (1978) and the Clarendon Centre (1986); a surviving gable on the right inspired three others during the 1980s.

A bus narrowly misses the duty policeman at Carfax as it swings round into St Aldate's, August 1925. Boffin's half-timbered baker's shop had a delightful first floor café where you could sit and watch the world go by. On the left, Wyatt's the drapers had lowered the shop blind to protect their stock from the afternoon sun.

Modern Carfax was created in the early 1930s when the south-east and south-west corners were set back and rebuilt in a rather chaste manner. Most traffic has been banned from Queen Street and Cornmarket since the early 1970s, but the long campaign to improve the city centre for pedestrians and cyclists is still being waged.

The upper end of St Aldate's opposite the Town Hall, August 1908. A striking row of eighteenth- and early nineteenth-century properties accommodated a wide range of businesses including Francis Matthews' photographic studio, Copsey's hair saloon (warm baths for 6*d*) and Eyles & Eyles' cycle shop.

Variety was replaced by uniformity in the 1930s as tall, neo-Classical offices were built opposite the Town Hall. The 'To Let' sign marks Therm House, erected in 1939 for the Oxford and District Gas Company. In the distance, Clarendon House (1956–7) supplanted the old Clarendon Hotel.

A lively scene outside Christ Church, probably during Eights' Week, *c.* 1900. The St Aldate's frontage of Christ Church was begun after 1525 when Cardinal Wolsey founded his college on the site of St Frideswide's Priory. It was left unfinished when he fell from power in 1529, and was only completed by Christopher Wren's Tom Tower in 1681–2.

Following refacing in 1964–5 the Christ Church front has a much sharper appearance and this is further emphasized by the absence of shrubs and climbing plants; the wall to the right of the façade was set back in the mid-1920s. Growing tourism is reflected by the heritage signpost, interpretation panel and litter bin.

St Aldate's looking up towards the Town Hall, *c.* 1900. The road still narrowed sharply as it approached the site of the long-demolished South Gate in the City Wall. The little shop beyond the entrance to Littlemore Court was the Sheep Shop where Alice (in Wonderland) Liddell bought her favourite barley sugar.

The creation of Christ Church Memorial Garden in 1925–6 widened the east side of St Aldate's and opened up new views of Christ Church and Tom Tower. On the west side, more subtle changes have included the removal of rendering from Littlemore Hall and the restoration of what is now known as Alice's Shop.

NORTH-WEST OF CARFAX

George Street, 1913

Newspaper House in New Inn Hall Street, June 1969. Erected in 1880, this tall brick building was originally Walter Higgins' furniture warehouse; in 1929, it was acquired by the Oxford Mail and Times and both titles were printed and published in these central, but increasingly cramped, premises until 1972.

The Oxford Mail and Times moved to Osney Mead in 1972 and North Bailey House was built on the site in 1974–5; beyond Shoe Lane, the gabled building now occupied by the Coventry Economic Building Society replaced the former St Michael's School in 1977. The southern end of New Inn Hall Street is now pedestrianized.

New Inn Hall Street, *c.* 1880, looking north past surviving medieval buildings of New Inn Hall which had been used as the royal mint during the Civil War. Beyond nineteenth-century student accommodation for the hall, there was a succession of churches: St Peter le Bailey (1874), Wesley Memorial (1878) and George Street Congregational (1832).

New Inn Hall was absorbed by Balliol College in 1887 and most of its medieval buildings were demolished for the Girls' Central School (1900) in the foreground. The school and adjoining properties, including the former St Peter le Bailey Church, are now part of St Peter's College (founded 1928). The George Street Congregational Church was pulled down in 1935.

Campaigners outside the YMCA in George Street, 1913. They planned to raise £2,500 in six days which would pay off outstanding debts on the building and provide a new suite of rooms for boys. Beyond Victoria Court, the New Theatre had been rebuilt after a fire in 1908.

The YMCA in Oxford is now only recalled by its ornate initials and the datestone 1891 above the Going Places shopfront; the building's exuberant roof line was lost after a serious fire in what had become the Clarendon Restaurant in June 1966. Further down George Street the New Theatre was rebuilt in 1933 and was renamed the Apollo in 1986.

Wintry weather in George Street, 1906. The Grapes pub, on the extreme left, was built in 1894 and its architect, Harry Drinkwater, designed it to blend in with its older neighbours. These buildings survived for only a few more years, however, and the demolition men were about to move in when this photograph was taken.

A change of scale, with the Grapes now dwarfed by four-storey properties erected between the late 1900s and 1939. The one-time toy warehouse nearest the Grapes was given a contemporary façade in the 1960s but was restored to something like its Edwardian appearance during refurbishment as the Wig and Pen in 1996.

Car parking in Gloucester Street, April 1965. Double Diamond was on sale at the Red Lion and non-alcoholic drinks at Burton's Milk Bar on the opposite corner. To the right, City Motors still occupied the garage and showroom where the firm began in 1919.

Gloucester Street is now a no-through road with parking discouraged, if not prevented! City Motors abandoned its central premises in the 1970s and the site was redeveloped by the Co-op in 1985. The dress designer, Anna Belinda's, has flourished in Gloucester Street since the mid-1970s and, following refurbishment in 1996, the Red Lion is now the Fuggle and Firkin.

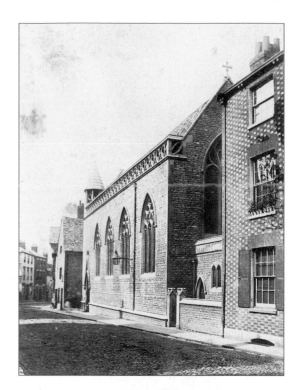

Looking west along a cobbled George Street, 1860s. On the right, St George's Church was built in 1847 as a district church in the parish of St Mary Magdalene following extensive house-building in the area.

A very different George Street, now closed to most through traffic and rapidly becoming a street of eating and drinking houses. St George's Church closed in about 1918 and became Oxford's Labour Exchange before being demolished in 1935 for the Ritz Cinema, now the ABC George Street. It is recalled by St George's Place in front of the cinema.

Gloucester Green cattle market in full swing, *c*. 1900. The brick building on the left was a settling room for market traders, built in 1881; beyond the pens, the seventeenth- and eighteenth-century houses on the north side of the Green were soon to be replaced by the Central Boys' School. The buildings of Worcester College are visible in the background.

The Wednesday market in a transformed Gloucester Green. Oxford's cattle market was moved to the Oxpens in 1932 and Gloucester Green became a bus station and car park in 1935. After years of debate, the area was redeveloped in 1987–9 to provide shops, offices, apartments, a bus station and an open space to which the market could return.

Country buses parked in Gloucester Green in 1959, most of them resplendent in the old City of Oxford Motor Services Ltd three-colour livery. The Greyhound pub is visible in the foreground with the buildings and gardens of Worcester College beyond Worcester Street; the tower of St Barnabas' Church (1872) rises above the trees.

The Gloucester Green coach station now occupies a smaller area and the entrance and exit for vehicles is in George Street. Four-storey offices in Worcester Street back on to the coach station and formed part of the Gloucester Green redevelopment scheme.

Two undergraduates add human interest to this view of Worcester College in the 1860s. The medieval south range of the Cistercian Gloucester College contrasts completely with the eighteenth-century library which formed one element of Worcester College's ambitious, but unfinished, rebuilding scheme.

Some dormer windows have disappeared from the Stonesfield slate roof of the south range and the hugely projecting lamps have been replaced by lights of more modest dimensions. The upper floor of the library has been refaced in Clipsham stone.

Worcester Street from the corner of George Street, looking towards New Road and the County
Education Offices, October 1954. Job's milk float waits at the traffic lights and obsolete signs nearby
recall Oxford's two railway stations and wartime Air Raid Precautions. Over the wall, contractors were
busy clearing the canal site.

Worcester Street was straightened and realigned to speed the flow of traffic and a surface car park was
provided on the site of the wharf. Demolition exposed to view the white painted former Queen's Arms,
now Rosie O'Grady's, and properties in Tidmarsh Lane. Nuffield College front was built in the late 1950s.

The Oxford Canal, looking north from Hythe Bridge, *c.* 1900. The absence of vegetation on the towpath confirms that horse-drawn narrow boats were still going to the wharf in New Road. Behind the two boys, an overflow weir drains surplus water into the Castle Mill Stream, a tributary of the River Thames.

Trees and shrubs have softened all the hard edges and the canal now ends beyond the windlass-like structure which was built to mark the bicentenary of the Oxford Canal in 1990. Access to the wharf south of Hythe Bridge Street was lost because Lord Nuffield bought the site in 1937 for his new college.

Middle Fisher Row, looking across Pacey's Bridge to Lower Fisher Row, c, 1885. This lively waterside community had developed on the Wareham bank between two branches of the Thames in the seventeenth century. The local people, picturesque houses, workaday punts, cobbled quaysides and festoons of washing attracted many artists.

The former Nag's Head pub on the right, now Antiquity Hall, was rebuilt in 1938. The rest of Middle Fisher Row was cleared in 1954 and converted into a public garden. Pacey's Bridge was rebuilt in 1925, forcing the pedestrian to climb steps and cross Park End Street on the level.

The Oxford Canal basin in New Road, 1930s, with neat stacks of coal ready for delivery; the Worcester Street wharf is visible in the distance. The old County Police Station can be seen in New Road and, away to the right, the gables of seventeenth-century houses in George Street Mews overlook the canal basin.

The view from the City of Oxford Conservative Club shows how Nuffield College, built between 1949 and 1958, filled the site of the canal basin. St Peter's College occupies the foreground with a car park and a garden which adjoins Canal House, now the Master's lodgings. Part of the canal boundary wall survives on the left beside New Road.

Two-way traffic in Park End Street, August 1962. Layton's garage on the corner of Tidmarsh Lane had just closed but Coxeter's and Hartwell's garages were still flourishing in Park End Street. Archer Cowley's huge furniture repository, built at the turn of the century, dominated the street beyond Coxeter's.

Park End Street became a one-way street in the 1960s and, as part of the City's Balanced Transport Policy, a bus lane was introduced in 1982. There are no garages left but most buildings have been converted to new uses; Coxeter's garage is now an antiques centre and Archer Cowley's premises house auction rooms, a nightclub and a second-hand bookshop.

A welcoming array of pubs including the Robin Hood and the Railway Hotel greet railway travellers in Rewley Road, August 1907. The traditional striped pole advertises William Best's hairdresser's shop and the eye is led down towards Hollybush Row past the brick entrance to an underground public convenience.

The busy junction of Hythe Bridge Street and Rewley Road seen here at a peaceful moment. The Royal Oxford Hotel replaced the older properties in 1935 and, off to the right, Frank Cooper's extended their Victoria Buildings to the corner of Hollybush Row in 1929. King Charles House occupied the other corner in 1992.

The old Great Western Railway station in Park End Street during severe flooding, November 1875. As an alternative to the cab, enterprising punt owners offered to ferry railway passengers across the street for a penny. In the background, the station, opened in 1852, still retained its original overall roof.

Patience is still a virtue in Park End Street but most of the waiting is now done in the vehicles which flood in and out of the city every day. The present Oxford station, visible beyond the bus shelter, was built in 1990 and the redundant water tower at the south end of the platform was removed in the 1970s.

Park End Street, with a horse tram waiting to take passengers from the railway stations to the city centre and Cowley Road, 1900s. Cooper's Oxford Marmalade is advertised on the tram and was manufactured nearby at Victoria Buildings, the four-storey structure beside the trees, which opened in 1903.

Traffic and road markings are now dominant features in Park End Street but the buildings have scarcely changed. Cooper's extended their premises across the site of the trees to Hollybush Row in 1929, but moved to the old Majestic Cinema in Botley Road in 1951. The Castle Hotel, now shorn of its distinctive chimneys, received its last guests in the mid-1950s.

The Headington bus successfully negotiates the Botley Road railway bridge, 1960s. Some Oxford buses were too high for the bridge and, although they were kept off this route, accidents sometimes happened; passengers were therefore advised to warn any driver who seemed to be heading for disaster.

A Park and Ride bus carries shoppers past the bridge which was rebuilt by British Rail in 1979. Although the headroom is nominally the same as it was thirty years ago, the clearance provided by the old bridge has been redefined in later years as 13ft 3in. The signal gantry is still in situ but the water tank was removed in the 1970s.

NORTH-EAST OF CARFAX

Broad Street, c. 1875.

Market Street and the Oxford skyline from the upper floor of the new Woolworth's store in Cornmarket Street, October 1957. Old properties in Market Street dating back to the 1840s housed a number of well-known businesses such as Wenborn's the cutlers, Strange's the ladies' hairdressers and Arthur Rowles & Sons, seedsmen and florists.

Today's view from Clarendon House, which Woolworth's left in 1983. Marks & Spencer expanded their new store on to the Market Street frontage in 1960–1 and the Oxford and Swindon Co-op took over the store in 1978; now subdivided, the building houses a number of shops and the Co-op Food Hall.

Turl Street and Lincoln College, looking north towards Broad Street, *c.* 1880. The Turl was still cobbled and a quiet place for two men to discuss the issues of the day. The fifteenth-century college front had been battlemented and regularized in the 1820s.

Turl Street remains a delightful Oxford backwater and, for vehicles, it is now a one-way street with restricted access. The Lincoln College façade has been refaced and a doorway has been cut through the wall on the right. The massive horse chestnut tree on the corner of Market Street gave way to Lincoln House in 1939.

Ship Street slumbers in the sun, *c.* 1865. Old town houses of the seventeenth and eighteenth centuries overlook Jesus College garden behind the stone wall. At the end of the street, Exeter College Chapel, designed by G.G. Scott and completed in 1856–9, towers above the Turl Street frontage of the college.

Saved from imminent demolition by the outbreak of war in 1939 the Ship Street houses have been happily preserved. To the right, Jesus College built the New Block in 1905–7, but a fine horse chestnut tree still adorns the street corner; at Exeter College, attic rooms lit by dormers have provided space for more students.

Workmen relaying cobbles outside the Broad Street shop of Henry Taunt, the Oxford photographer, *c.* 1880; Taunt occupied these premises between 1874 and 1895. Neighbouring businesses included Thornton's bookshop (established 1835) to the left and Neill's the opticians on the right.

This attractive range was a candidate for redevelopment before the Second World War, but it is now appreciated as a foil for grander college and university buildings. A model shop for many years, Taunt's old premises are now occupied by Oxford Campus Stores, but Thornton's still flourishes at no. 11.

Perfect peace in Broad Street, *c.* 1875. Just a few carts occupy the centre of the street but there would have been many more on market days. Opposite, the seventeenth-century Trinity Cottages contrast with Waterhouse's Gothic range for Balliol College, built in 1867–8.

Car parking took over the centre of Broad Street in 1926 despite complaints from Parker's Bookshop that customers would no longer be able to see the shop above the car roofs. Trinity Cottages were reconstructed in 1967 and Balliol still dominates the town houses opposite. Tall Victorian-style lampposts now illuminate the street at night.

Blackwell's bookshop and adjoining premises in Broad Street, *c.* 1910. B.H. Blackwell founded his well-known business at 50 Broad Street in 1879 and expanded into no. 51 in 1883. The cab and bicycles outside were perhaps awaiting the return of browsers in the bookshop.

Blackwell's is now a worldwide business, but nos 50–1 Broad Street are still superficially the same. The adjoining nos 48–9 were rebuilt as an extension for Blackwell's in 1938 and, since 1966, these deceptively small shopfronts have led to 3 miles of shelving in the basement of the Norrington Room.

The decayed stonework of the Sheldonian Theatre and the Clarendon Building, *c.* 1880. The original seventeenth-century Emperors' heads in front of the Sheldonian and the Old Ashmolean had been replaced by new ones in 1868. To the right, the Broad Street front of Exeter College had been built in two stages, in the 1830s and in 1856.

Parked cars now dominate the foreground but restoration since the 1960s has left these historic buildings in fine condition. The Emperors' heads had to be renewed again in 1972, and all the lead statues are now in place on the Clarendon Building.

The former Seal's Coffee House on the corner of Broad Street and Holywell Street, 1882. Dating from the early eighteenth century, this impressive building had been a private house since 1844. It was due for demolition and the crowd outside was probably attending the sale of building materials held that day.

The Indian Institute was built on the site in 1883–5 and was extended southwards by two bays in 1894–6. Since 1976 the building has housed the History Faculty Library, but exterior details recalling its original purpose include Hindu demigods and the heads of tigers and an elephant.

The junction of Broad Street and New College Lane from Catte Street, *c.* 1900. This early morning view looks past the Clarendon Building and the white-painted King's Arms into Parks Road. The tiny house with two dormers to the left of the lamp-post was a radical conversion of the early sixteenth-century Chapel of Our Lady at Smith Gate.

Hertford College bought the corner site in 1898 and it was cleared to make way for T.G. Jackson's North Quad, built between 1903 and 1931. The only building to survive was the little chapel which Jackson restored and rebuilt in 1931. On the left, the planted enclosure has gone, providing a glimpse of the New Bodleian Library (1937–40).

The fourteenth-century gatetower of New College framed by soot-stained medieval walls, 1907. The original Warden's hall and chamber were above the arched doorway, giving him complete oversight of all comings and goings. These rooms had been lighted by inappropriate sash windows since about 1800.

Double yellow lines provide the only incongruously modern note in a still ancient scene. The stonework of New College gatetower has been restored and old-style windows have replaced the sashes. Niches on the upper floor contain statues of the Virgin Mary flanked by an angel and the kneeling college founder, William of Wykeham.

Parks Road and Wadham College, January 1936. Built between 1610 and 1613, Wadham brought a new classical symmetry to the traditional collegiate style; some decayed Headington stone had already been replaced by this date. A few cars have intruded on the scene but bicycles predominate in Parks Road.

Wadham College was refaced in Clipsham stone in 1957–66 and now looks as crisply new as it must have done in the reign of James I. More cars now take advantage of the on-street parking, and a cycle lane has been added in Parks Road to improve conditions for Oxford's many cyclists.

The University Museum from the south-west, 1880s. Built between 1855 and 1860 to provide facilities for science teaching, the museum was bitterly opposed by conservative factions within the University, and its Gothic style was denounced by Tennyson as 'perfectly indecent'.

The University Museum is now at the heart of an extensive science area in South Parks Road. The west wing of the Radcliffe Science Library, added in 1933–4, intrudes a little, but when a further extension of the library was needed in 1976 it was put underground to preserve the green setting of the Museum.

Undergraduates peer from the windows of the old Dolphin Inn in St Giles', *c.* 1875. The Dolphin dated back to the sixteenth century and housed students in its later years; the bars on the ground floor windows deterred potential criminals and restricted the freedom of the undergraduates and their friends to come and go as they wished.

The neo-Georgian Dolphin Quad of St John's College (1948) replaced the inn and the stonework of the older college buildings has been restored. Revolving spikes on top of the linking wall made life difficult for locked-out undergraduates until the more liberal 1960s. In the foreground, an old cabbies' hut (of *c.* 1910) has been converted into a little shop.

The southern end of St Giles' with many horse-drawn cabs awaiting passengers, *c.* 1880. Behind the inquisitive figure in the foreground tall elm trees survived to the south of St John's College; the elms on the left had been replaced by plane trees in the late 1850s.

A busier St Giles' with traffic lights, road markings and much-needed pedestrian refuges. An extension to the Ashmolean Museum was built beyond the Taylorian Institute in 1932. Taxis still wait in the centre of St Giles', but a slip road to Magdalen Street East has replaced the elms.

SOUTH-EAST OF CARFAX

Corpus Christi Quad, c. 1870.

The Bear and Blue Boar Street, 1901. The original Bear Inn stood on the corner of High Street and Alfred Street and this pub, formerly the Jolly Trooper, only became the Bear in 1801. Blue Boar Street was named after an inn in St Aldate's and still retained a number of old properties facing south over Christ Church.

Large-scale floral displays welcome visitors to the Bear which has become famous for its collection of ties built up since 1952. Houses further along Blue Boar Street have been pulled down, exposing the side wall of Ebor House, the former home of the city's Chief Constable. On the left, the Blue Boar Quad of Christ Church (1968) now overtops the wall.

Horse-drawn cabs outside the Canterbury Gate, the monumental back entrance to Christ Church, *c.* 1880. James Wyatt's building, erected in the 1770s, was blackened by soot but much less decayed than the older buildings of Oriel College and Corpus Christi College to the left of the picture.

Oriel Square is now a parking place for cars and bicycles. Restoration and cleaning of old stonework since the 1960s has transformed the scene, leaving two badly eroded gatepiers as the only relics of a shabbier Oxford. Beyond the Canterbury Gate, Corpus added an unobtrusive modern building in 1957–9.

Oriel College and the distant spire of St Mary the Virgin Church, *c.* 1870. The gatetower and one gable had been restored but the seventeenth-century façade was otherwise in a scabrous state typical of Headington stone. Below the Bear Lane name plate, William Hinton ran a confectioner's business.

A profusion of bicycles outside today's extensively restored Oriel College. The southern end of Oriel Street was widened when King Edward Street was laid out in 1870 and it is now known as Oriel Square. The northern section, robbed of business by King Edward Street, soon lapsed into peaceful slumber and is now closed to through traffic.

The sixteenth-century Front Quad of Corpus Christi College, *c.*1870. The unknown photographer managed to persuade five people to pose around the famous Turnbull sundial (1579) which is topped off by the college's pelican. The sundial was fenced off from the mid-eighteenth century, probably to deter climbers.

Three current students stand beside the sundial, which lost its railings in 1936 and was meticulously restored to its early eighteenth-century appearance in 1976. The Front Quad no longer has its battlements but it gained dormer windows which light extra rooms in the attics; it was refaced in the 1960s and paving was introduced in 1972.

Progress claims old houses on the corner of Merton Street and Grove Street, now Magpie Lane, *c.* 1884. The second property was the George and Dragon pub; further along, the four-gabled house was the western part of Beam Hall, rebuilt in 1586.

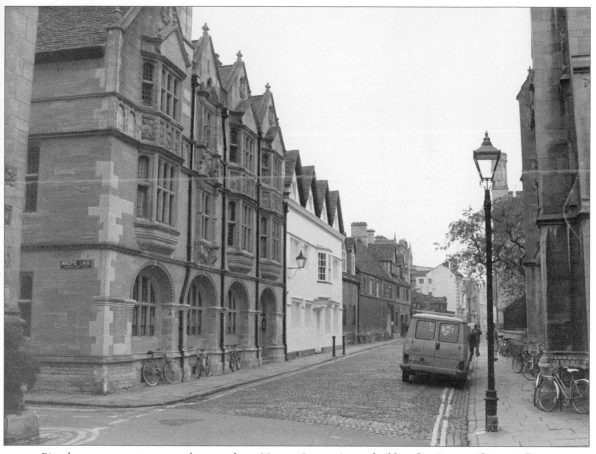

Bicycles now seem to outnumber people in Merton Street. A new building for Corpus Christi College, designed by T.G. Jackson, occupied the corner site in 1884–5, but Beam Hall and other old buildings have changed remarkably little. The cobbled road surface was retained after a struggle in the 1960s and old-style lanterns provide the street lighting.

Magpie Lane, looking south towards the fifteenth-century tower of Merton College Chapel, *c.* 1900. Two rows of early nineteenth-century houses on the left are interrupted by the entrance to Kybald Street and an old stone building. The Oriel College boundary wall occupies the right-hand side.

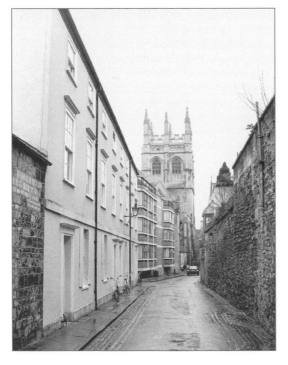

Magpie Lane is an almost timeless part of Oxford, changed only by the ubiquitous yellow lines and, beyond Kybald Street, by the New Building (1969) which provided thirty-six study bedrooms for Corpus Christi College.

A conversation is interrupted outside Merton College, *c.* 1880. The College gateway dates back to 1418, but the rest of the frontage was gothicized in 1836–8; St Alban Hall, with the prominent gables, was incorporated into Merton in 1881. Further on, huge horse chestnut trees billowed out across Merton Street from the Fellows' Garden.

The street frontage of Merton College has been cleaned and restored but, beyond the two distant pedestrians, prominent chimneys distinguish St Alban's Quad, a rebuilding of the old St Alban's Hall by Basil Champneys in 1904–10. The number of bicycles shows that most students find two wheels essential.

A top-hatted visitor inspects the Oxford Botanic Garden, *c.* 1860. Behind the formal beds, the two-storey house had been created out of a former orangery in 1848 to provide a home for Charles Daubeny, Professor of Botany (1834–57). Magdalen College bell tower, built between 1492 and 1509, completes the view.

Much less formality is now evident in this part of the Botanic Garden. Daubeny's House has been refaced and the conservatory to the right is an aluminium replica of an earlier timber one; the conservatory nearest the entrance was ruinous by 1911 and has been removed.

SOUTH-WEST OF CARFAX

High Street, St Thomas's, 1907.

Castle Street and the New Road junction, after Macfisheries had left the corner shop, August 1968. Old properties in Castle Street, some dating back to the seventeenth century, were being cleared for the Westgate development. On the left, behind the bus queue, customers were still pounding the wooden floors of Cooper's department store.

The Westgate Centre from Bonn Square, named after Oxford's twin city in 1974. Built across the ancient alignment of Castle Street, the Westgate development was completed in 1973 and included a new central library. The gabled structure beyond the flower stall was built in 1986 when the echoing shopping arcade was closed in and upgraded.

Watched by a policeman, a 100ft crane hauls one of a number of compressor units on to the roof of the City Chambers, June 1967. They formed part of an air-conditioning system for the City Treasurer's new computer. Three Oxford businesses from another era, Cooper's, Cape's and Starling's, were still flourishing in St Ebbe's Street.

St Ebbe's Street is now a pedestrian precinct and bicycle park. It was quickly transformed in the early 1970s as Cooper's gave way to Selfridge's, Cape's to Fenwick's and Starling's to a branch of Barclay's Bank and student accommodation. All those businesses have gone in their turn and St Ebbe's Street is forever changing.

Undergraduates fill the entrance to Pembroke College, *c.*1870. Pembroke was founded in 1624 and the Old Quad had been built in the classical style in the seventeenth century. The gatetower and adjoining ranges, tucked away behind St Aldate's Church, were gothicized in 1829–30.

Pembroke's exuberant battlements, chimneys and gatetower parapet were shaved off during a late Victorian restoration by Bodley and Garner. On the right, a former doorway has been cleverly converted into a window.

Beef Lane, looking east towards St Aldate's, July 1907. A street of humble timber-framed houses with rendered lath and plaster walls nestles in the shadow of Pembroke College's Chapel Quad.

Pembroke College built the Besse Building in the foreground in 1956 and took over the rest of Beef Lane in the 1960s. The site was then cleared to form the College's North Quad which incorporated a fine range of town houses in Pembroke Street. Retained street lamps are a reminder of the old Beef Lane.

Littlegate Street, looking north, July 1907. The tall seventeenth- and eighteenth-century house on the left, partly hidden by shrubs and creepers, was the vicarage for nearby Holy Trinity parish; beside a drinking fountain installed to encourage temperance in the 1850s, tattered notices encouraged men to spend an improving hour in church.

Holy Trinity House has been refurbished as St Aldate's Rectory, but the drinking fountain was removed and lost in the 1960s when the garden wall was breached for a garage entrance. The rest of Littlegate Street bears the hallmarks of 1970s redevelopment.

Friars Street and Commercial Road, looking west from the Albion pub, *c.* 1938; part of the Friars, an area of tightly packed terraced housing built in the early nineteenth century. A horse-drawn delivery cart is emerging from Wood Street, and Stanley Rogers' confectionery shop in Commercial Road is clearly visible.

Blighted by years of uncertainty, St Ebbe's was cleared in the 1960s and early 1970s, leaving few residents in a parish which once had an overcrowded population of over five thousand. Cars park on the site of the Albion (demolished 1980) but, further on, brick houses in Faulkner Street brought people back to the area in the 1980s.

Friars Wharf and the Wharf House pub, 1959. The Wharf House was built in about 1830 beside a wharf which extended north from the main river. When the railways destroyed most commercial river traffic in the early 1840s the wharf was filled in and the site was covered by houses.

Houses beyond the Wharf House were demolished in the 1960s to make way for Thames Street, a new route through St Ebbe's from Folly Bridge to Oxpens Road. New homes were built beside the pub in 1980–1 and brick houses occupied vacant land beyond Thames Street in 1979–80; they were built behind earth banks to reduce the effects of traffic noise.

Blackfriars Road, looking past Sadler Street and the old Mason's Arms pub, 1963. The road, laid out in the 1810s, ended abruptly at a branch of the River Thames, and it was nearly a century before a children's playground was provided on the far bank; the area was dominated in every sense by the Oxford gasworks.

West of Trinity Street, even the course of Blackfriars Road was lost when this part of St Ebbe's was redeveloped in 1979–80. Sadler Walk, recalling the former Sadler Street, leads past attractive brick houses and luxuriant planting to a riverside walk.

Paradise Square, with Castle Street in the distance, March 1965. Built between 1838 and 1847, Paradise Square was a late and never really fashionable addition to St Ebbe's. The fencing on the left marked the boundary of St Ebbe's School, which shared the centre of the Square with the Rectory.

In distant Castle Street two small houses of about 1700 can still be seen, but the Westgate multi-storey car park replaced the east side of Paradise Square in 1974; even the street name, Norfolk Street, has been changed. On the left, Tennyson Lodge (1996) stands on the site of St Ebbe's School.

High Street, St Thomas's, when many local people were keen to be in the picture, September 1907. Many of the attractive timber-framed houses were pubs or lodging houses, and behind the street frontage dozens lived in squalid and overcrowded yards. Local employers included Cooper's Bakery on the left and, in the background, Morrell's Brewery.

Slum clearance before and after the war removed every old property in what is now known as St Thomas's Street, opening up views of St George's Tower (1074) and Morrell's Brewery. In recent years housing has begun to make a welcome return, and developments include The Old Bakery (1995) on the left.

JERICHO & NORTH OXFORD

Banbury Road, 1900s.

Little Clarendon Street, looking east, when the concrete-framed Fry–Nuffield building at Somerville College was transforming this neighbourhood shopping centre, 1966. Traditional shops in Victorian premises included Eakett's boot repairing business, Allen's the fruiterers and Wyeth's cycle shop.

The south side of Little Clarendon Street was largely redeveloped in the 1970s for university offices and student accommodation above shops. Fashionable boutiques and shops offering 'presents and gifts from five continents' were attracted to the street which became known as Little Trendy Street.

Great Clarendon Street, looking east from Hart Street, April 1974. These typical early Jericho houses of rendered timber framing or brick were erected very soon after this area was laid out for building in 1825. The portico of St Paul's Church, built for the new district in 1836, is visible in Walton Street.

St Barnabas' School moved to new premises in Hart Street in 1977 and the Great Clarendon Street houses had been demolished in 1976 to make way for the school's playing field. The street is still overhung by a yew tree and St Paul's Church, derelict in 1974, is now Freud's café bar and restaurant.

The proud occupants of 37 Great Clarendon Street when Rose sent this picture postcard to her friend Elsie Hudson in Reading, *c.* 1907. It seems likely that Rose was one of the women in the doorway and placed the advertisement for Miss Heiden, Dress Maker in the front room window. The little brick house has an enamel street name plate and a tiled window box.

The same street name plate still announces Great Clarendon Street at its junction with Albert Street. No. 37 now has a painted brick front and a modern door; its original small-paned sash windows were probably replaced soon after 1907.

Demolition in progress in Nelson Street, Jericho, 1976. These houses were built in the 1840s and had attractive façades of red and grey brick with sash windows. Some were as little as 9ft wide, however, and the rooms were tiny.

The rebuilt section of Nelson Street alongside the retained no. 22. The development respects the scale and the character of the older Jericho houses even if the brickwork and windows do not have quite the same charm.

Cranham Street, looking east from Cranham Terrace, *c.* 1910. Beyond the Radcliffe Arms pub and Norman Cummings' grocer's shop brick terraced houses of the 1860s extend up the slope towards Walton Street, the local shopping centre for Jericho.

This part of Cranham Street was cleared in the 1960s, leaving only the Radcliffe Arms which now has a painted brick façade. New flats, including Grantham House on the right, replaced the terraced houses in the early 1970s, but the Victorian shop on the far side of Walton Street still terminates the view.

Woodstock Road, looking north from the Horse and Jockey pub when North Oxford was being transformed from a series of fields into a high-status suburb, *c.* 1870. SS Philip and James' Church had been built in 1860–2 and, behind traces of old boundary hedge, the Holy Trinity Convent (1868) was newly finished.

Woodstock Road with a bus and cycle lane to beat rush hour traffic jams. The Horse and Jockey is still visible on the left but the former SS Philip and James' Church, now the Oxford Centre for Mission Studies, is almost hidden by trees. The convent added a chapel, marked by a spire, in 1894 but St Antony's College took over the whole site in 1964.

Marston Ferry Road, looking east towards Cherwell School, August 1967. The road regained its rural character at this point continuing as a track to Marston Ferry. The City and County Bowls Club, marked by the sign of an ox, moved here in the 1930s, and Cherwell School opened as a secondary modern in 1963.

Marston Ferry Road became a through route between Summertown and Marston in 1971 following the completion of the long-awaited Marston Ferry link road. Improved accessibility has probably helped to increase the popularity of Cherwell School, which is now perhaps the city's most popular comprehensive school.

Banbury Road near Oakthorpe Road, 1900s. A woman cyclist has the road to herself as she heads for the city centre; behind her a horse tram travels up to the South Parade terminus. By the turn of the century, red brick villas had filled the gap between suburban North Oxford and Summertown village.

Traffic lights create a momentary lull in what is now a busy main road. The loss of a tree on the right has exposed the former Diamond Terrace, built perhaps in the 1850s, which has become a parade of shops south of the main Summertown shopping centre. Technology has rushed on from the age of the telegraph to the installation of cable telecommunications.

Woodstock Road, Summertown, north of the Woodstock Arms pub, 1940s. Wartime is suggested by some of the messages on the hoardings and by the lightless street lamp with white paint around its base. The woman waiting for a bus does her best to blot out austerity with a cigarette.

The poster site and adjoining properties made way for Ridgemont Close in 1972. Other nineteenth-century buildings have survived and, beyond the Woodstock Arms, the 1930s Red Lion pub is now the Lemon Tree restaurant.

Part of the Summertown shopping centre, December 1959. Rising's toy shop, described as 'a children's paradise', was a new venture for the firm which had run a nearby electrical goods shop since the 1930s. Weeks' confectionery business next door and Butler's baker's shop were local branches of well-known Oxford firms.

Rising's continues to flourish in a busy Summertown shopping centre, where firms have had to sacrifice some of their forecourts and pavement display space to make room for customer car parking. The origin of all these shops as turn-of-the-century villas is still evident above the shopfronts.

ST CLEMENT'S & EAST OXFORD

The Plain, 1912.

Hall's Oxford Brewery drays at The Plain, May Day 1912. The parade of drays through central Oxford became a regular feature of May Day at the turn of the century and promoted a thriving brewery that had taken over several smaller firms in the 1890s. The memorials in the background were in the old St Clement's churchyard.

The Plain has been adapted to cope with growing traffic levels. The area was reshaped as a roundabout and the churchyard memorials were removed in 1949–50, but the retention of mature trees, some with mistletoe, still gives The Plain a special character. The Waynflete Building of Magdalen College (1960–1) is visible through the trees.

High Street St Clement's, looking towards Headington Hill, *c.* 1900. This was the main shopping centre for the little streets between the River Cherwell and Cowley Road. It included Kempson's the fruiterers in the foreground and, beyond the entrance to Penson's Gardens, the tiny Star pub and the Bon Marché, an outfitter's shop.

Side streets like Penson's Gardens have gone but St Clement's Street itself has hardly changed. Kempson's closed down in 1977 and is now a restaurant; Electric Aids has taken over the Star and a music shop occupies the former Bon Marché. The pedestrian crossing shows that the road is rarely as quiet as this.

Toys in the gutter at Little Brewery Street, St Clement's, *c.* 1930. Six ashlar stone cottages built perhaps in the 1820s are in the shadow of Wootten's Brewery. The quiet street was the children's playground, but the houses lacked basic facilities and were in a poor state.

Two- and three-storey houses with car parking spaces were built in Little Brewery Street in the 1980s. Part of the gradual rehabilitation of St Clement's since the 1970s, these properties offer a degree of luxury beyond the wildest dreams of earlier residents.

Superior council houses nearing completion at the foot of Morrell Avenue, *c.* 1930. They formed part of the South Park estate, which was built between 1929 and 1931 on land acquired from the Morrell family at Headington Hill Hall. The neo-Georgian houses were designed in the City Engineer's Office by Kellett Ablett.

Nos 2–12 Morrell Avenue still offer a civilized welcome to Oxford visitors descending Headington Hill. Apart from limited re-windowing the houses are little changed.

Shopping by bicycle in Cowley Road, December 1957. Wiggins' was an old-established shop selling bicycles and electrical goods, and had boasted a cycle riding school in the 1890s. Other local businesses included Rayburn's the outfitters and, beneath the shop blinds, the tobacconist Patrick Devlin and Cocks' general store and post office.

Wiggins' old shop is unlet, symbolizing the difficulties of local traders as their more mobile customers are lured further afield. Beyond the launderette, a post office still flourishes at no. 129.

Cowley Road opposite the former Cowley Road Workhouse when petrol rationing had reduced traffic levels, April 1941. Beyond Slatter & Rose's, Pickett & Sons were wireless dealers, with tall aerials outside the shop to improve reception. Strips of tape on the windows were to prevent flying splinters of glass in the event of an air raid.

The busy Cowley Road is now best crossed by the pedestrian crossing in the foreground. This shopping parade selling food from all over the world reflects the cosmopolitan character of modern East Oxford. On the right, the solitary pine tree marked the entrance to Cowley Road Hospital until that was demolished in 1985; now it stands on the corner of Manzil Way.

Cowley Road, looking east past Rivera, the home of Oxford photographer Henry Taunt, July 1914. Taunt acquired this property in the late 1880s, and after he gave up his shop in central Oxford he urged customers to visit him here 'Five minutes beyond the Tram Terminus, at the big Aspen Tree'.

A decidedly urban Cowley Road including what Taunt described as a White City of council houses built on the right in 1920–1. Glanville Road was laid out in the foreground in 1923 and just two years after Taunt's death in 1922 City of Oxford Motor Services Ltd built its bus garage on his land. Despite all the changes, Rivera survives as 393 Cowley Road.

Iffley Road, looking towards Iffley Turn from the corner of Donnington Lane, 1920s. On the left, hundreds of allotments occupied the fields leading down to the Boundary Brook; on the right, beyond the entrance to Donnington House, council houses in Freelands Road are visible through the trees.

Today's busy junction, controlled by traffic lights since the building of Donnington Bridge in 1962. The boundary wall of the demolished Donnington Lodge survives on the right but, beyond Donnington Bridge Road, Townsend Square occupies the site of Donnington House. On the left, interwar housing and Boundary Brook Road have supplanted the allotments.

The Free Ferry footbridge over the Thames, looking towards Long Bridges, as the crew of an eight hauls its boat back to a nearby boathouse, 1950s. A free ferry was provided here from 1897 to take East Oxford residents across to the Long Bridges river bathing place; the elegant concrete footbridge put the ferryman out of work in 1937.

A road between South and East Oxford was proposed in the early 1920s, and it was at last achieved in 1962 when Donnington Bridge was opened; the redundant Free Ferry footbridge was subsequently demolished. The plain surfaces of Donnington Bridge have proved irresistible to the daubers of Eights' Week and other graffiti artists.

SECTION EIGHT

SOUTH & WEST OXFORD

Abingdon Road during floods, 1875.

An exciting moment at Salter's Yard as a lifeboat filled with brave souls plunges into the river, June 1900. The event, watched by hundreds, was the climax of a fund-raising Lifeboat Day in Oxford. In the background, the Oxford Folding Lifeboat was waiting its turn to be launched.

The Head of the River pub now provides everyday entertainment at Folly Bridge. Salter Bros, the Oxford boatbuilders, vacated the site in the early 1970s and the impressive stone buildings dating from 1827 were converted into a pub in 1977. New buildings on either side accommodate undergraduates.

Swans on the river near Folly Bridge, 1960s. The stone building on the left housed the City Waterworks between 1826 and 1854 and was later part of a City Council depot. Nearer to Folly Bridge, mid-nineteenth-century houses took little advantage of the enviable river frontages.

Today's fashionable Oxford riverside arose almost by accident following the clearance of the Isis Street area in the early 1970s and the failure of a gargantuan hotel scheme. After a lengthy delay, the site was occupied in the 1980s by the houses and flats of Folly Bridge Court.

Folly Bridge weir and distant St Ebbe's, *c.* 1868. Despite heavy flooding the Thames towpath and the old Great Western railway line running north to the river are still visible above the water. A wooden bridge in the middle distance carried the towpath over the Hog Acre Ditch.

The course of the river and a surviving Victorian house on Folly Bridge island are the only constants in a much-altered scene. Houses gradually filled the low-lying meadows south of the river from the late 1870s. In the foreground, Waterman's Reach occupies the site of old wooden boathouses.

The industrial Thames next to St Ebbe's, January 1925. Basson's Baltic Wharf on the left still received regular boatloads of timber from the London Docks, while narrow boats from the Oxford Canal brought coal to the gasworks opposite and collected waste products from the manufacture of town gas.

A very different river, transformed since the closure of the gasworks in the 1960s and the subsequent clearance of the site. The three-storey houses on the right were built in 1979–81 as part of the St Ebbe's redevelopment scheme. Pembroke College built a new quad, the Sir Geoffrey Arthur Building, on the Baltic Wharf site in 1987–90.

Vicarage Road, looking east towards Abingdon Road from the corner of Gordon Street, 1960s. The cheerful boys were probably returning from an outing to New Hinksey School further along the street.

The same view today with more parked cars and no sign of schoolchildren. A few new properties have been slotted in, and most of the small mid-nineteenth-century terraced houses have been modernized with painted fronts and new windows; in many cases redundant chimney pots have been removed.

New council houses near completion in Weirs Lane, 1920s. These houses were being built on land that the City Council had bought from University College. On the right, the house with an almost flat roof was one of a pair of paper houses built in the nineteenth century for workers at the nearby Weirs paper mill.

Council housing on the south side of Weirs Lane replaced the old paper houses in about 1930. The lane led down to Weirs Mill, and it remained a cul-de-sac for vehicles until Donnington Bridge was completed in 1962.

Floods at Cold Harbour on the Abingdon Road when a punt provided public transport, 1875. The view is looking north past early nineteenth-century houses called the Saltboxes, towards the Fox and Hounds pub on the corner of Weirs Lane.

Horsepower makes a brief comeback in Abingdon Road during a gap in the traffic. Rivermead Hospital was built as the City's Isolation Hospital in 1886 and distant white chimneys mark the Fox and Hounds, which was rebuilt in 1926. On the left, the brick-built houses are part of the Hinksey Glebe council estate built in about 1930.

South Street, Osney, under water, early 1900s. Osney Town, developed close to the city's railway stations in the 1850s, was nicknamed Frogs' Island because residents were forced by regular flooding to become virtually amphibious. In this case, planks provided narrow pavements and a punt was available for crossing the street.

With more effective flood prevention, flooding no longer poses a regular threat to Osney Town. South Street looks much the same but, on the right beyond Bridge Street, flats replaced the former St Frideswide's School in the 1960s. Pylons dominate the far end of the street, bringing electricity to a substation in Ferry Hinksey Road.

Botley Road, looking towards Oxford from the Botley or Seacourt Bridge, early 1920s. There is no apparent traffic problem but a sign on the pavement warns motorists of a 10mph speed limit, which had been imposed in central Oxford in 1910 to curb furious driving.

Botley Road was improved in 1923–4, partly to relieve local unemployment, and it attracted both commercial and residential development before the war. The Seacourt Park and Ride car park on the left was opened in 1974 to deter shoppers and commuters from driving into Oxford; superstores on the right encourage other motorists to join the daily queues.

THE OXFORD VILLAGES

Cowley, 1900s.

Mill Road, Old Marston, looking north past the village pond, *c.* 1885. The Parliamentarians held Marston during the siege of Oxford in 1646, and the treaty surrendering the city was signed at the distant Manor House, or Cromwell House. The old house had been rebuilt with two different façades in the 1840s.

The local ducks are now pondless and the thatched building has given way to modern houses. On the bend, gabled dormers and an extension were early twentieth-century additions to Cromwell House; the Manor House to the right is little changed.

Marsh Lane, Old Marston, during the building of the Boult's Farm housing estate, September 1967. Wimpey homes were nearing completion beside the road which led to the Northern Bypass and the still elmy landscape between Old Marston and Elsfield.

The view today from the corner of Elms Drive. The maturing trees on the roadside verges provide some compensation for the lost elms in the background.

Old High Street, Headington, looking south from the famous elm tree, 1900s. This was the heart of the old village, with the post office on the right and outbuildings belonging to the Black Boy pub behind the tree. The lime or linden trees in the distance gave their name to the adjacent house, The Lindens.

Apart from the parked cars the view has changed little. The half-timbered Linden Cottages were built on the left in 1909 and the Black Boy corner was set back in 1937. The fine old tree has given way to broken lines marking the junction with St Andrew's Road, and the former post office is a private house.

New High Street, when local custom supported a general drapery store, *c.* 1900. New Headington dates from the early 1850s and the four brick terraced houses beyond the draper's would have been built soon afterwards; further along, the gable of New Headington's first Methodist Church (1889) is just visible.

The drapers has gone, the row has been extended by one house, and rendering has masked bricks which almost certainly came from Headington brickworks. On the right, the entrance to All Saints' Church House has replaced a luxuriant hedge and shops have supplanted trees in distant London Road.

London Road, looking east past Headington Carfax, 1900s. The trees on the left mark the boundary of the Headington House estate which still extended right down to the main road. The Oxford Co-operative Society opened its shop on the corner of London Road and Windmill Road in 1892, initiating commercial development in this part of Headington.

The heart of Headington shopping centre, which developed quickly between the wars as the local population increased. New shops, banks and other premises were built and old properties like the terraced houses beyond the phone box were converted to retail use. The Co-op shop is now an estate agents.

Football fans stream out of Headington United's Manor Ground, and turn London Road into an unofficial pedestrian precinct, 23 March 1957. United began as a village football team in 1893, and it was only in 1949 that the club turned professional and joined the Southern League.

Headington United became Oxford United in 1960 and the club was elected to the Football League in 1962, winning the Milk Cup in 1986. London Road has changed surprisingly little but, at the end of a Nationwide Division One game, the fans look very different and the police are out in force.

Barton village, showing the Prince's Castle pub with Barton Manor and a row of picturesque thatched cottages stretching away up the hill, *c.* 1900. The signboard of another pub, the Fox, is just visible on the last building. On the left, a fine old farmhouse rises behind an ancient rubble wall.

The Northern bypass effectively cut off Barton from the rest of Headington in the 1930s and led to the demolition of the Fox. In 1946, Barton became the site of a huge council housing estate and most of the area's historic buildings were destroyed. The former Prince's Castle pub survives, however, and Barton Manor has been rescued from utter dereliction.

A peaceful North Way looking towards Marston from Barton Road, mid-1950s. Part of the Northern bypass, this two-lane road extended for 9 miles from Headington to Eynsham and was built in 1930–5; it took through traffic on the A40 out of central Oxford.

The 1930s road is now the westbound carriageway of a dualled Northern bypass, which carries heavy traffic between the often congested Banbury Road and Green Road roundabouts. A cycle lane, originally omitted from the city stretch of the road in the 1930s, provides cyclists with a safe route to old Marston.

Horwood's Pit in Headington Quarry, 1900s. Stone quarrying in Headington is recorded from the late fourteenth century, but use of the local freestone declined because of its poor weathering qualities and this pit was the last working quarry in the area. The house above the pit probably dates back to the eighteenth century.

Scrutton Close now occupies the site of Horwood's Pit with the older house, now known prosaically as 24 Beaumont Road, visible in the background on a higher level. These bewildering changes of level resulting from centuries of quarrying give Headington Quarry a character of its own.

Children outside Headington Quarry Church of England School, March 1906. Their 'hand me down' clothes and pinched expressions reflect the contemporary poverty in Quarry where most households needed a secondary income if they were to subsist.

Ninety years on, some of today's Quarry schoolchildren stand with their teacher outside the same door; trainers have replaced hob-nailed boots in a tarmac playground. The stone building is little changed externally but the tiled roof is in better condition and more effectively drained.

The Slade, when the City Council was beginning to improve it and to introduce gas street lighting, July 1933. Little more than a country lane, The Slade was becoming increasingly built up and also formed an important link between the growing areas of Headington and Cowley.

Traffic levels in The Slade have justified a pedestrian crossing near the junction with Girdlestone Road. The properties at the head of Lye Valley are still recognizable, but a 1930s council estate is evident further along and, to the left, Slade Close dates from the 1950s.

A boy shows off the massive ruts in Crescent Road, Cowley, 1906. The British Land Company laid this road out in the 1860s as a speculation but, despite the views over Oxford, builders were reluctant to invest in plots. The building in the distance may have been connected with the Oxford Military College which had a sports field at the top of Crescent Road.

The varied housing of Crescent Road reflects the gradual development of vacant sites over many years. Salesian Close, leading off to the right, recalls the former Salesian College which, in 1921, took over buildings erected for St Kenelm's School (1880) and the Franciscan College (1906).

The Stocks Tree in Oxford Road, looking up towards the Waggon and Horses and, further away, the Original Swan, 1900s. A printed notice on the tree directs visitors to the Church Army Press, which had been established in Temple Road in 1903. A barn belonging to White's Farm can be seen behind the tree.

The modern junction of Oxford Road and Temple Road, lacking the Stocks Tree which was felled in 1907. White's Farm gave way to flats in 1957 and the tower of the now redundant St Luke's Church (1938) looms above the trees. On the right, Cedar Court (1996) occupies the long-vacant site of the Waggon and Horses and other old houses.

Between Towns Road looking towards Garsington Road, when many local children were clearly happy to have their picture taken, 1900s. There was enough space in one of the Victorian terraced houses for the old Cowley post office. In the distance, part of the old Oxford Military College can be seen, with the Original Swan pub away to the right.

A totally different Between Towns Road, now a dual carriageway and dominated on the left by a 1960s office block. W.R. Morris acquired the Military College buildings in 1912 for the production of his Bullnose Morris; later, as car making expanded, the Nuffield Press took over the site and added the prominent extension facing Garsington Road in 1931.

Garsington Road, late 1930s, showing part of the huge Morris Motors assembly plant which transformed Cowley and indeed Oxford between the wars. The two distant chimneys, masked by camouflage paint during the Second World War, were local landmarks until 1993.

The landscaped Oxford Business Park in Garsington Road with a distant view of the remaining Rover plant on the Pressed Steel site. The old North and South Works were closed down in 1992 and the gigantic site was subsequently cleared, leaving nothing but memories. The Nuffield Needle on the roundabout was erected to keep those memories alive.

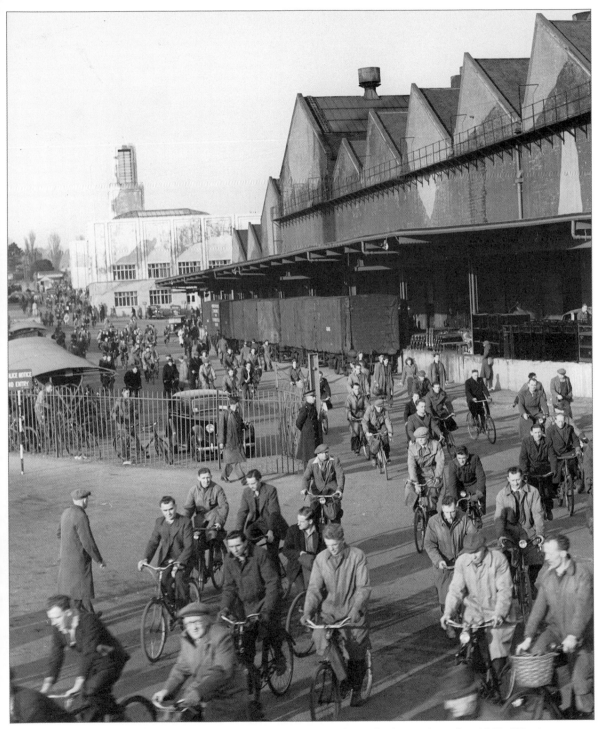

Dozens of cyclists pour out of the Pressed Steel site at the end of a working day, 1950. Wartime camouflage is still evident on 'A' Building and the Company's office building. In 1959, Oxford's Eastern bypass was built between Pressed Steel and the Morris works at this point, filling a gap left for the purpose by pre-war planners.

The Rover sign beyond a modernized 'A' Building is fixed to the remains of the overhead conveyor which carried vehicles from the Assembly Plant in the old Morris factory to the Body Plant. A flyover now carries the Eastern bypass over Garsington Road and the roundabout in the foreground is for local traffic.

Oliver Road in Cowley, looking west towards a distant Wilkins Road, 1930s. Part of the Sunnyside private housing estate built after 1931, Oliver Road was one of many similar streets providing comfortable semi-detached houses with gardens for Oxford's fast-growing population between the wars.

Growing car ownership has brought pavement parking to Oliver Road and some front gardens have been sacrificed to provide off-road parking space. Electric street lighting has replaced the old gas lamps.

Children play on and around the fountain which was a central feature in The Square in the new Cowley Centre, 1965. The brand new branch of Webber's Oxford store is visible in the background and Ward's also opened a Cowley shop. National businesses attracted to the Centre included W.H. Smith's, Sainsbury's and Woolworth's.

The fountain, usually out of order and litter-strewn, became a sad symbol of the run-down shopping centre in the 1970s and 1980s. During the rebirth of Cowley Centre as Templar's Square in 1989 the windswept shopping malls were given glazed roofs, and a café and display area now occupy the site of the fountain.

Hockmore Street from the junction of Crowell Road, *c.*1960. Old Cowley village houses on the right give way to the offices and gable end of John Allen and Son, the local agricultural engineering business founded in 1868. Beyond Rymers Lane a semi-detached house is representative of hundreds built in Cowley during the 1930s.

The semi-detached house and the gable end survive but old Hockmore Street was swept away by the Cowley Centre development. John Allen's, latterly Grove Allen's, closed down in 1985 and the site was redeveloped in 1987 as a retail park called the John Allen Centre; B&Q was one of the major businesses atttracted to the new Centre.

Cowley Road, Littlemore, with a motor-cyclist hurrying towards the village past a row of modern semis, 1920s. The girls on the left were standing at the corner of Van Dieman's Lane; seemingly remote places had often been named after distant Van Dieman's Land, the modern Tasmania.

This part of Littlemore no longer seems very remote, with housing on both sides of the road and fewer trees in evidence. Hedges have been retained in front of many of the houses and, beyond the posts, a row of chestnut trees survives at the beginning of Van Dieman's Lane.

Sandford Road, Littlemore, looking past the George pub towards the distant Marlborough Head on the corner of the Cowley and Oxford roads, *c.* 1916. Part of the main road between Oxford and Henley, it had clearly been levelled over the years, leaving an embankment beside the footway which was an ideal lounging place.

Relieved of through traffic by the bypass in the 1960s, Sandford Road is quiet again. The George and adjoining properties are easily recognizable, but the loungers' embankment has gone and a double garage has replaced the pair of houses on the right. In the distance, the Marlborough Head pub was rebuilt on a larger scale in 1940, but has now been converted into flats called Blewitt Court.

Railway Lane, the former Church Way to Iffley, looking towards Laburnum Farm, 1903. The three people in the photograph seem stiffly posed, or were perhaps transfixed by the muddy road and the fear of getting their boots dirty.

Laburnum Farm was burned down in 1951 when a spark from a passing locomotive lodged in the thatch. Railway Lane now leads down to an oil depot and the premises of Littlemore Scientific Engineering Co., but the concrete kerbs seem to echo the lines of the earlier verge and footway.

Church Way, Iffley, near the Prince of Wales pub, 1911. Three pedestrians keep confidently to the middle of the road as they round the corner. The house on the left, Rivermead, may date back to Elizabethan times; the block on the right, including a shop, seems to have been up for sale.

Iffley post office and village shop flourishes on the right and the Prince of Wales has merely changed its allegiance from Hall's to Wadworth's. Parked cars tend to dominate the scene, but the houses have scarcely changed and Iffley still retains the character of a village.

Iffley Mill and Lock, *c*. 1900. First recorded in 1160, the picturesque water-mill was a favourite subject for artists and early photographers. Iffley Lock, on the left, was one of the first pound locks on the River Thames, built in 1632.

Iffley Mill was burned down on 27 May 1908 and was never rebuilt. Iffley Lock, which had long been criticized as a cause of flooding in Oxford, was rebuilt in a different position in 1924. Covered bridges above two weirs carry a footpath from Iffley to the lock.

The Southern bypass with a fingerpost pointing towards South Hinksey, late 1930s. The two-lane road from the foot of Hinksey Hill to Botley, promptly dubbed 'The Road from Nowhere to Nowhere', was opened in 1932 as an early part of the Oxford Ring Road. During the war it was used as a store for military vehicles.

The Oxford Ring Road was eventually completed in 1965 and, with the growth of traffic, the Southern bypass was dualled in 1973. Extended southwards as part of the Abingdon bypass in 1973 and now linked to the M40, the road is part of the A34 and a very busy link in the national road network.

Plenty of boats for hire at Medley, *c.*1910. Two old Oxford families touted for business here, the Bossoms on the left bank and the Beesleys on the Port Meadow side. Both used an ingenious network of rafts and houseboats to extend their dominions across the Thames, virtually preventing through traffic on the river.

Medley's rowing boats have been ousted by moorings for cruisers and converted narrow boats, reflecting the popularity of holidays on the Thames and the canal network. Beyond the boats, the wide open spaces of Port Meadow stretch away to distant Wolvercote.

The Perch and Manor Farm at Binsey, *c.* 1950. The thatched inn with its flagged floors and oak beams was still quite rustic and unpretentious. In this low-lying meadowland near the Thames, the floodwater in front of Manor Farm shows how Binsey, meaning Byni's island, got its name.

Binsey remains a preciously remote corner of Oxford, but the Perch had to be rebuilt after a fire in 1977 and inevitably lost some of its ancient charm. An extensive car park has spruced up the entrance and the flood-prone land in front of the farm has been raised, probably to deter illicit parking.

Godstow Road in Lower Wolvercote, *c.* 1910. Victorian infilling, both terraced and semi-detached, combined with older houses to produce a varied charm. The thatched cottages in the distance probably dated back to the seventeenth century.

The thatched cottages were demolished as slums in the 1930s, opening up a distant view of the green; on the right, a detached brick house with lions on the gateposts replaced an old timber-framed property. Beyond the rubble wall on the left, a modern brick wall marks the boundary of Webb's Close, a development of flats built in the 1960s.

Mill Road, *c.* 1900, showing eighteenth-century houses on the left and, on the right, a group of cottages which were probably built for paper mill workers in about 1860. Beside the bicycle, a door gave access to the Mill House, the side wall of which was completely smothered in creeper.

Beyond the modern paper mill offices which are just visible on the right the Mill Road houses have scarcely changed. The post and rail barrier outside the cottages has given way to more individual solutions and the side wall of Mill House is now exposed. A tarmac road and street lighting are obvious improvements.

Woodstock Road roundabout, February 1936. The building of the A40 Northern bypass involved the formation of junctions with the old main roads to Banbury and Woodstock. In this view, telegraph poles march on towards Woodstock and the brick parapet of the Oxford–Bletchley railway bridge is visible behind two standing figures.

An unusually good time to approach the Woodstock Road roundabout, which is a daily bottleneck for commuters. The street furniture and road sign have been updated and the roundabout is now attractively planted. Beneath the road sign there is a glimpse of the City Motors garage, relocated from the city centre to this busy site in the 1970s.